STEAM IN SOUTH WALES

Series Index

Compiled by
Michael Hale
and Tony Miller

Published by The Wider View

Introduction

The six volumes that make up the Steam in South Wales series contain just over 1,100 photographs, most of which were taken in the late 'fifties and early 'sixties, a time of great change. In the early part of this period locomotives of the pre-grouping companies could still be found at work, while the new British Railways standard types were being introduced. Diesel traction was displacing steam on shunting duties in goods and marshalling yards, but the next decade brought about a tremendous drop in the need for such duties. Diesel multiple-units made their appearance in the valleys but some services remained steam-worked until their withdrawal.

Diesel locomotives - some with hydraulic, others with electric transmission - increased in numbers while redundant steam locomotives could be seen in dumps awaiting disposal, many at private scrapyards. With the implementation of Dr. Beeching's policies, withdrawal of services and the closure of stations and goods yards gathered momentum. Steam working on British Railways' lines in South Wales came to an end in 1965.

The photographs in the series provide an almost complete record of that period, the final years of steam. The vast majority of stations are illustrated, together with examples of lineside structures such as goods sheds and signal boxes. The various types of locomotives, the depots where they were serviced and some of the men who worked them are featured. It is hoped that this Index will enhance the value of the six volumes as a work of reference for future historians.

Michael Hale
Dudley
April 1999

Contents

General notes on the series	3
Explanatory notes on the use of the Index	3
Rail network coverage by volume	4
Errata and amendments	6
Index of historical notes	7
Index of locations	8
Index of plates showing signal and signal boxes as a prominent feature	16
Index of plates showing notices, lineside furniture	16
Index of plates showing locomotives	17

Copyright © 1999 Michael Hale & Tony Miller.

ISBN 0 9535848 0 1

British Library Cataloguing in Publication Data.
A catalogue record for this book is available from the British Library.

All rights reserved. No part of this book may be reproduced or transmitted in any form or by any means, electronic or mechanical including photocopying, recording or any information storage and retrieval system, without written permission from the Publisher.

Edited and typeset by Tony Miller, Great Gidding.

Printed in Great Britain by Stylaprint, Elton, Cambridgeshire.

Published by The Wider View,
2 Luddington Road, Great Gidding, Huntingdon, PE17 5PA.

Distributed by the Welsh Railways Research Circle,
22 Pentre Poeth Road, Bassaleg, Newport, NP10 8LL.

Front Cover:

(Upper) This unusual somersault signal, possibly of Brecon & Merthyr Railway origin, was photographed at Bargoed Colliery.

11th June, 1962

(Lower) One of F.W.Hawksworth's taper-boilered pannier tanks, No.8414, heads an up goods along the main line near Baglan Loop signal box.

16th April, 1960

Rear Cover:

Llanharry station, on the former Taff Vale Railway Cowbridge branch, closed from 26th November, 1951, but this stretch of line remained in use until 28th July, 1975, when the ironstone quarry closed. Standing at the head of a train of hoppers bound for East Moors, Cardiff, 0-6-0PT No.3656 is gently blowing off.

26th August, 1959

Plate 1

Disposing of a steam locomotive after its turn of duty was not a glamorous operation, as these piles of ash and clinker testify. Waiting to go on shed at Aberdare are Nos.6361, 3753, 4688 and 7204.

4th June, 1963

Preamble

The first four volumes in the Steam in South Wales series were not indexed in any way, nor were the pages numbered although, fortunately, each photograph was given a Plate number. The Welsh Railways Research Circle maintained the style and format when it published volumes five and six. Thus it is that just over 1,100 monochrome and 27 colour plates - including those on the dust-wrappers - are entirely un-indexed beyond their Plate numbers.

As well as pictures, Michael Hale also included many paragraphs containing historical information about the railways and the locations he photographed. The precise whereabouts of that valuable information, too, is un-indexed.

The purpose of this book is to remedy the situation by indexing the locations photographed, historical notes and, as an added extra, most of the locomotives shown in the photographs.

Numbering Convention

References are quite simply given using a Volume number and the appropriate Plate number.

Roman numerals are used to identify a Volume, ordinary numbers to identify Plates; ie. a reference to III-78 is Plate 78 in Volume Three; VI-2 is Plate 2 in Volume Six.

There are, however, two principal departures from that convention:

     a. Firstly, the use of IDX to reference the Plates in this Index volume;

     b. Secondly, the use of the letter J in place of a Plate number to show that the photograph is on the dust-jacket.

When there is more than one reference to a specific subject in a volume, the second and subsequent references do not carry the volume number:

     eg. Cardiff - East Dock Shed III-30, 31, 179, VI-178, 179.

Coverage of Volumes I to III and Section Listings

The books were not divided into recognisable chapters but they did include sub-sections, some as short as a single page, others quite extensive. Since the geographical coverage of the different volumes overlapped in many places, a single map depicting the lines included in each volume would be over-complicated and difficult to unravel.

Thus a listing is provided of the sections in each volume, referenced by the Plate numbers to aid location.

Volume I
The Valleys
Oxford Publishing Company 1980

Eastern Valleys	Plates 3-8
Western Valleys	9-19
Sirhowy Valley	20-22
Heads of the Valleys	23-29
Brecon & Merthyr Railway	30-46
Cardiff Railway	47-49
Rhymney Railway	50-61
Taff Bargoed branch	62-65
Taff Vale Railway	66-80
Rhondda Valleys	81-95
Merthyr	96-102
Ely Valley	103-105
Mid-Glamorgan Valleys	106-125
Colour plates	118-121
Port Talbot Railway	126-130
Rhondda & Swansea Bay Railway	131-140
Colour plates	141-144
Vale of Neath	145-166
Dulais Valley	167-173

Volume II
North and West of Swansea
Oxford Publishing Company 1981

Swansea	Plates 2-4
Landore	5-8
Morriston branch	9-13
Swansea District line	14-17
To Llandilo	18-24
Branches to Brynamman	25-36
Brynamman	37-39
Midland to Swansea	40-47
To Llanelly	48-58
Llanelly	59-63
Llanelly area	64-91
Carmarthen	92-103
To Newcastle Emlyn	104-107
Carmarthen LNWR branch	108-113
Llandilo to Swansea	114-118
Carmarthen to Whitland	119-123
Pembroke & Tenby	124-136
Cardigan branch	137-148
Lines through Haverfordwest	149-155
Neyland	156-159
Milford Haven	160-162
To Fishguard	163-174
Fishguard	175-180

Volume III
Main Line and the Docks
Oxford Publishing Company 1982

Newport Dock	Plates 2-13
Newport Main Line	14-23
Cardiff Docks	24-27
Cardiff East Dock	28-39
To Barry	40-74
Vale of Glamorgan	75-83
Cardiff Main Line	84-93
Llantrisant area	94-105
Bridgend	106-107
Pyle to Porthcawl branch	108-118
Margam	119-122
Port Talbot	123-128
Briton Ferry	129-139
To Swansea Docks	140-164
Main Line to Swansea	165-173
Swansea (High Street)	174-177

Plate 2

A Neyland engine at that time, 4-6-0 No.4983 Albert Hall takes the evening West Wales to Kensington milk through Llangennech and heads for the Swansea District Line.

31st July, 1958

Coverage of Volumes IV to VI and Section Listings

Volume IV
Monmouthshire
Oxford Publishing Company 1984

Pontypool Road	Plates 2-6
To Newport	7-21
To Blaenavon	22-38
Main Line	39-45
Severn Tunnel Jct to Chepstow	46-55
Wye Valley Railway	56-67
Monmouth to Little Mill	68-81
To Abergavenny	82-89
Heads of the Valleys	90-104
Sirhowy Valley	105-118
Western Valleys	119-160
Brecon & Merthyr Railway	161-168
To Rhymney (B&M)	169-172
Taff Vale Extension	173-184

Volume V
East & Mid Glamorgan
Welsh Railways Research Circle 1996

Merthyr Tydfil	Plates 2-4
To Quakers Yard	5-8
GWR/RR Joint	9-17
Abercynon	18-21
To Aberdare	22-28
To Ynysybwl	29-34
Rhondda Valleys	35-51
To Cardiff	52-68
Cardiff Railway	69-79
Rhymney Railway	80-82
Caerphilly area	83-99
To Senghenydd	100-104
To Rhymney	105-123
LNWR to Merthyr	124-133
Brecon & Merthyr Railway	134-148
Barry Railway	149-162
To Llantrisant	163-165
Ely Valley	166-170
To Gilfach Goch	171-173
Ogmore Valley	174-180
Garw Valley	181-184
Tondu	185-190
Llynvi Valley	191-194

Volume VI
The General Scene
Welsh Railways Research Circle 1999

Severn Tunnel Junction	Plates 2-5
Pontypool, Caerleon & Newport Railway	6-9
Western Valleys	10-16
Vale of Neath line	17-51
Rhondda & Swansea Bay Railway	52-67
Neath & Brecon Railway	68-76
Swansea Vale & N&B Jct Railway	77-78
Swansea Vale line	79-83
Swansea	84-87
Pembrey & Burry Port	88-92
Llanelly	93-101
Swansea District line	102-109
Neath	110-112
Porthcawl branch	113-117
Port Talbot Railway	118-140
Tondu	141-148
Bridgend	149-152
Llantrisant	153-156
Barry lines	157-162
St. Fagans and Ely	163-164
Tanks in the Valleys	165-168
Cardiff General	169-172
Cardiff East Dock	177-181
Cardiff Canton	182-185
Newport Dock area	186-191

Plate 3

The site of Robertstown Halt on the Ynysybwl branch was marked by a Taff Vale Railway trespass notice and a McKenzie & Holland signal post bearing two fixed distant arms.

25th August, 1959

Plate 4

Merthyr shed was opened in 1877 and improved in 1932. The engines visible in this yard scene are Nos.82043, 6436, 6433, 4616, 9765 and 9636.

6th April, 1958

Errata

Volume One

Plate 31   - amend date to 3rd July, 1965

Plate 39   - locomotive number should read 9662

Plate 65   - amend date to 5th August, 1956

Plate 71   - train was 12.46pm to Merthyr

Plate 74   - amend date to 2nd August, 1958

Plate 92   - should begin "Through a nominally....."

Plate 103   - amend date to 5th April, 1958

Plate 104   - amend date to 5th April, 1958

Plate 105   - amend date to 5th April, 1958

Plate 113   - amend name to Brynmenyn

Plate 128   - amend date to 26th August, 1959

Plate 133   - better to say "branch to join the South Wales Mineral Railway", and the collision occurred to the south-west of the station

Plate 155   - Penrhiwceiber Low Level was on the Taff Vale line

Plate 161   - duties included banking to Hirwaun Pond

Plate 171   - amend date to 14th July, 1956

Plate 173   - branch should read Maes y Marchog

Volume Two

Plate 2   - amend date to 22nd April, 1962

Plate 16   - amend date to 27th August, 1959

Plate 17   - amend date to 27th August, 1959

Plate 97   - the 0-6-0 number should read 2294

Volume Three

Plate 154   - "It is now..." should read "It is not..."

Plate 166   - amend date to 28th July, 1958

Plate 177   - name should read St. Fagans Castle

Volume Four

Plate 71   - insert "to Usk" after NAHR

Volume Five

Plate 3   - amend withdrawal date to 31st December, 1962

Plate 8   - the new road runs on the other side of the valley, and this is a small housing estate

Plate 23   - name should read Mathewstown

Plate 39   - road was the A4058

Plate 52   - plate number omitted

Plate 149   - amend line closure date to 8th March, 1962

Plate 150   - amend withdrawal date to 10th September, 1962

Plate 154   - through trains from Treforest to Cadoxton continued until 17th June, 1963

Plate 193   - for Blaengwynfi read Abergwynfi

Plate 5
The sun has just broken through after a downpour as 0-6-0PT No.3641 arrives at Pantyffynon with the 7.01pm to Swansea.

25th July, 1960

Historical Notes on Railway Companies, Places, etc.

Alexandra (N&SW) Docks & Railway	III-2
Barry Railway	III-45, 83, V-153
Brecon & Merthyr Railway	IV-166, 170, V-139
Cardiff Railway	I-47, III-24
Coleford, Monmouth, Usk & Pontypool Railway	IV-71
Cowbridge Railway	III-96
Duffryn Llynvi & Porthcawl Railway	III-110
Llanelly Railway	II-18, 25, 109, VI-93
Llanelly & Mynydd Mawr Railway	II-65
Llynvi Valley Railway	V-192
Margam Yard	III-119
Merthyr, Tredegar & Abergavenny Railway	I-26, IV-90, V-128
Merthyr Tydfil	V-2
Monmouthshire Railway	IV-13, 22
Neath & Brecon Railway	I-167, VI-68
Ogmore Valley Railway	V-174
Pembroke & Tenby Railway	I-124
Pontypool, Caerleon & Newport Railway	VI-6
Pontypridd, Caerphilly & Newport Railway	V-52
Port Talbot Railway	III-122, VI-137
Radyr	V-61
Rhondda & Swansea Bay Railway	VI-55
Rhymney Railway	I-50, V-105
Severn Tunnel	IV-45
Sirhowy Valley Railway	I-21
South Wales Railway	II-2, III-16, 84
South Wales Mineral Railway	I-137
Swansea District Line	VI-106
Swansea Harbour Trust	III-148, 154
Swansea Vale Railway	II-39
Swansea Vale & Neath & Brecon Junction Railway	VI-76
Taff Bargoed	I-62
Taff Vale Railway	III-43
Taff Vale Extension	VI-19
Vale of Neath Railway	I-96, 145, VI-36
Whitland & Cardigan Railway	II-146

Index of Locations

A

Aber Junction   V-100, 101
Aberaman   I-92, 95
Aberavon Seaside   III-127
Aberavon Town   I-131, VI-57, 58, 59
Aberbargoed   IV-171, 172
  - Junction   IV-168
Aberbeeg I-12, 13, 17, IV-127, 128, 135, 136, VI-13, 14
  - shed   I-16
Abercanaid   V-11
Abercarn   IV-142
Abercynon   I-91, V-18, 19, 20
  - shed   V-21
Aberdare
  - Dare Valley Junction   V-28
  - Gadlys Junction   VI-31
  - High Level   I-157, 159, VI-30
  - Low Level   V-26, 27
  - shed   I-143, 158, IDX-1
Aberdulais   I-165
Aberfan   V-10
Abergavenny
  - Brecon Road   IV-91
  - GWR shed   IV-84
  - Junction   IV-87, 90
  - LNWR shed   IV-92
  - Monmouth Road   IV-85, 86
  - Usk bridge   IV-93
Abergwili   II-108
  - Junction   II-99
Abergwynfi   I-125
Abernant   VI-35
Abersychan & Talywain   I-7
Abersychan Low Level   I-4, IV-27
Aberthaw   III-76
Aberthin   III-99
Abertillery   IV-133
Abertridwr   V-103
Alberta Place   III-51
Ammanford   II-26
  - Ammanford Colliery   II-25
Argoed   IV-112

B

Bargoed   V-117, 118
  - Colliery   IV-169
  - South Junction   V-115, 116

Barry
  - Docks   III-59
  - harbour sidings   III-66
  - Island   III-67, 69, 70, 71, VI-158, 159, 160, 161
  - Pier   III-73, 74
  - shed   III-61
  - Town   III-60
  - Woodham's yard   III-65
  - Works   III-63, 64
Bassaleg   I-33
  - Junction   IV-152, VI-10
Beaufort GWR   IV-121
Beaufort LNWR   IV-101
Beavers Hill   II-132
Bedlinog   I-62, V-16
Bedwas   I-40, IV-165
Bedwellty Pits   I-22
Berw Road   V-32
Birchgrove   V-71
Bird in Hand Junction   I-153
Blackmill   V-174, 175, 177
Blackwood   I-20
Blaenavon High Level   I-8, IV-36
Blaenavon Low Level   I-6, IV-J
Blaengarw   I-114, 121, V-184
Blaengwynfi   I-135, 136
Blaenrhondda   VI-69
Blaenycwm   VI-68
Blaina   IV-131, VI-15
Boncath   II-146
Bournville Mon   IV-132
Branches Fork Junction and shed   IV-24, 25
Bridgend   I-106, III-107, VI-150
  - Coity   I-107, 108
  - Cowbridge Road Junction   III-106
Brithdir   V-119
Briton Ferry   III-128, 129, 130, 131, VI-55, 56
Brockweir   IV-61
Bronwydd Arms   II-J, 100
Bryn   VI-136
Brynamman East   II-39
Brynamman West   II-37, 38
Brynmawr   I-26, 27, 28, 29, IV-99, 100
Brynmenyn Junction   I-113, V-180, VI-147
Burry Port   II-70, 73
  - shed   II-71, VI-91
Bynea   II-52
  - Birds' yard   II-53, 54

C

Cadoxton	III-57, 58
Cadoxton Terrace	VI-71
Caerau	V-193
Caerleon	IV-9, VI-6
Caerphilly	I-52, 53
- Beddau Loop Junction	I-119, V-93
- East Junction	V-86
- Watford Crossing	V-92
- Wernddu	V-83
- Works	I-50, 51, V-84, 85
Caldicot	IV-51
Cardiff	
- Adam Street Goods	VI-174
- Bute East Dock	III-32, 178
- Bute Road	III-38, 39
- Canton shed	III-87, VI-183, 186
- Clarence Road	III-36
- Dock Storage South	III-26
- East Dock shed	III-30, 31, 179, VI-178, 179
- Flat Crossing	VI-181
- General	III-84, 85, 86, VI-169, 170, 171, 172
- Leckwith Junction	III-90
- Newtown Goods	III-35, VI-174, 175
- Ninian Park	III-88, 89
- Northeast Junction	III-27
- Penarth Curve	III-40
- Pengam Junction	III-24, VI-176
- Queen Street	I-66, V-J, 68
- Riverside Platform	III-37
- Roath site	III-25
- Stonefield Junction	III-28
- Tyndall Street Crossing	III-34
- Tyndall Street Junction	III-33
Cardigan	II-148
Cardonnel	III-142
- Junction	III-143
Carmarthen	II-92, 93, 96, 98
- Junction site	II-95
- shed	II-97
Cathays Woodville Road	I-67
Cefn Coed	V-132
Cefn Coed Colliery	VI-73
Cefn Junction	VI-121
Cefn On	V-80, 81
Cefntilla	IV-77
Celynen North	IV-140
Celynen South	IV-141
Chapel of Ease Crossing	VI-129
Chepstow	IV-53
- bridge	IV-54
Cherry Orchard	V-82
Church Road	IV-163
Church Village	V-162
Cilfrew	VI-71
Cilfynydd	V-33
Clarbeston Road	II-151, 152, 163
Clydach	IV-96
Clydach Court	V-29
- Junction	VI-166
Clydach on Tawe	II-44
Clynderwen	II-149, 150
Clyne	I-164
Coed Ely	I-105
Cogan	III-44, 45
Colbren Junction	VI-77
Common Branch Junction	V-164
Conwil	II-101
Copper Works Junction	III-123, VI-127
Cornelly	III-111
Coryton	I-47, V-74
Court Sart	III-135
- Junction	III-132, 133
Cowbridge	III-100, 101, VI-156
Craiglon Bridge	II-76
Creigiau	V-151
Cross Inn	V-165
Cross Keys	IV-144, 145
Crumlin	
- High Level	IV-180
- Junction	I-147
- Low Level	IV-139, VI-12
- viaduct	I-148, 149
Crymmych Arms	II-145
Crynant	I-171, VI-73
- New Colliery	VI-74
Cwm	IV-125
Cwm Bargoed	V-15
Cwm Glyn	I-146
Cwmavon	VI-58
Cwmavon Mon	IV-28
Cwmbach	I-156
Cwmbran	I-3, IV-13, 14
Cwmcarn	IV-143
Cwmdu	I-130
Cwmffrwd	I-5
Cwmffrwdoer	IV-30
Cwmgorse	II-33, 34

Cwmmawr   II-82
Cwmsyfiog   I-44
   - Colliery   IV-170
Cylla   V-109, 110
Cymmer   I-134, V-194, VI-62, 63
   - Corrwg   VI-64
Cymllynfell   VI-83
Cynheidre Colliery   II-91
Cynonville   VI-62

D

Dafen branch   VI-99, 100, 101
Darran & Deri   V-147
Derwydd Road   II-23
Dillwyn & Brynteg   VI-75
Dinas Powis   III-46
Dinas Rhondda   V-45
Dingestow   IV-72
Dingle Road   III-49
Dowlais
   - Cae Harris   I-63, 64, V-12
   - Cae Harris shed   I-65
   - Central   I-99
   - Central shed   V-139
   - High Street   V-128
   - Junction   V-13
   - No. 1 Junction   V-138
   - Top (B&M)   V-140
   - Top (LNWR)   V-126, 127
Drope Junction   V-149
Drysllwyn   II-111
Duffryn
   - Mills   VI-134
   - No. 1 Junction   VI-130
   - No. 2 Junction   I-127, VI-133
   - No. 3 Junction   VI-128
   - Yard shed   I-141
Duffryn Isaf   V-160
Duffryn Rhondda   VI-61
Dynevor Junction   III-140, 144

E

East Usk Junction   IV-42
Ebbw Vale
   - High Level   IV-102
   - Low Level   IV-120
   - Sidings South   IV-123
Efail Isaf   V-152
Elms Bridge   IV-73

Ely Main Line   III-91
Ely Paper Mills   VI-164

F

Felin Fran   II-14
   - East   II-15, VI-108
   - West   II-13, VI-106, 107, IDX-9
Ferndale   I-81, 82
Ferryside   II-89
Ffairfach   II-24
Fishguard
   - & Goodwick   II-176
   - Goodwick shed   II-175, 179
   - Harbour   II-177, 178
Fleur-de-Lys   I-41, 42
Fochriw   V-144
   - Junction   V-142, 143
Fountain Bridge   I-J, V-88
Furnace Sidings   IV-37

Plate 6
The afternoon goods from Cardigan to Whitland is seen near Boncath, double-headed by 2-6-2Ts Nos.4557 and 4558.

1st September, 1959

G

Garnant	II-28, 29
Garndiffaith Junction	IV-33
Gelli Felen	IV-98
- tunnel	IV-97
Gelli Junction	VI-65
Gelli Tarw Junction	VI-33
Gellyrhaidd Junction	V-168
Genwen Junction	VI-103
Gileston	III-77
Gilfach Fargoed	V-114
Gilfach Goch	V-172, 173
Gilwern	IV-95
Glanamman	II-27
Glanyllyn	V-77
Glascoed	IV-79, 80
Glogue	II-144
Glyn Abbey	II-78
Glyn Neath	I-161, 162, VI-41
Glyncorrwg	I-J, 137, 138
Glyntaff Interchange Sidings	V-99
Golden Grove	II-112
Golynos Junction	IV-34
Govilon	IV-94
Gowerton North	II-57
Grangetown	III-42, 43
Groesfaen Colliery	V-148
Groeswen	V-97
Grovesend Colliery Loop	VI-105
Gurnos	II-40, 41
Gwaun Cae Gurwen	II-32, 35, 36
Gwernydomen	V-87
Gwys	VI-82
Gyfeillon Lower Junction	V-37

H

Hafodyrynys	I-142, IV-181
- Colliery	IV-182
Hall's Road Junction	IV-146
Haverfordwest	II-153
Heath	
- High Level	I-48
- Low Level	V-70
- Junction	V-69
Hendreforgan	V-170, 171
Hendy Junction	II-49, 50
Hengoed High Level	VI-17, 18
Hengoed Low Level	V-112
Henllan	II-106

Heol-y-Sheet Crossing	III-110, VI-114
Heolgerrig	V-134
Hirwaun	I-160
- Junction	VI-36
Hirwaun Pond	VI-37
Hollybush	IV-110

J

Jersey Marine	VI-46
- Junction South	III-146, VI-45
Johnston	II-154, 155
Jordanston	II-174

K

Kenfig Hill	V-187
Kidwelly	II-88
- East	II-87
Kidwelly Flats	II-85
Kilgerran	II-147
Kilgetty	II-126

L

Lamphey	II-133
Lando	II-84
Lavernock	III-53
Letterston	II-168
- Junction	II-169, 170
Lewistown	V-176, VI-147
Little Mill Junction	IV-81
Llanarthney	II-110
Llanbradach	I-57, V-105
Llandaff	V-64
Llandaff Loop Junction	V-63
Llandarcy	III-145
Llandebie	II-22, 116
Llandenny	IV-76
Llandilo	II-114, 115
Llandilo Bridge	II-113
Llandilo Junction	II-55, 59
Llandogo	IV-62
Llandow	III-81
Llandow Wick Road	III-80
Llandyssul	II-105
Llanelly	II-60, 67
- Morfa Junction	VI-94
- North Dock	VI-97
- Old Castle Crossing	II-68
- Sandy Junction	II-64, 65, VI-98
- shed	II-61, 62, 63, VI-93, 95, 96

Llanfalteg	II-139
Llanfyrnach	II-143
Llangefelach	II-16
Llangeinor	V-181
Llangennech	II-51, VI-102, IDX-2
Llanglydwen	II-141
Llangynwyd	I-123, V-189
Llanharan	III-102, VI-152
Llanharry	III-97, IDX-J
Llanhilleth	IV-137, 138
Llanishen	I-49
Llanpumpsaint	II-102
Llansamlet	III-169
Llantarnam	IV-6, VI-7
Llantrisant	I-103, III-95, VI-153, 155
- shed	III-96, VI-154
Llantwit Major	III-79
Llantwit Vardre	V-163
Llanvihangel Mon	IV-88
Llanwern	IV-43
Llanycefn	II-164
Lletty Brongu	VI-139
- viaduct	VI-138
Llwydcoed	VI-34
Llwynypia	V-48
Login	II-140
Lonlas Junction	VI-87
Loughor	II-58
Lower Cwmtwrch	VI-81
Lower Penarth	III-52
Lower Pontnewydd	IV-5
Lydstep	II-130

M

Machen	I-35, 36, 37, 38
Machine Sidings Junction	IV-129
Maenclochog	II-165
Maerdy	I-83
Maesaraul Junction	V-166
Maesteg Castle Street	I-124, V-191
Maesteg Neath Road	VI-136
Maesycwmmer	IV-166
Magor	IV-44
Maindy	V-66
Manorbier	II-131
Margam	III-119, 120, 121
- Middle	VI-124
- Sorting Sidings	VI-123
- West	VI-126

Marine Colliery	I-15
Markham Village	IV-111
Marshfield	III-23, IV-39
Mathewstown	V-23
Mathry Road	II-173
Melyncourt	VI-42
Merthyr	I-96, V-J, 3
- Brandy Bridge Junction	I-98
- Mardy Junction	V-135
- Plymouth Street	V-2
- shed	I-97, IDX-4
Merthyr Vale	V-7
Milford Haven	II-160, 161, 162
Monmouth	
- May Hill	IV-71
- Troy	IV-68, 69, 70, 185
Morlais Junction	VI-104
Morlais Tunnel Junction	V-131
Mountain Ash Cardiff Road	VI-29
Mountain Ash Oxford Street	V-25
Mwyndy Junction	V-167

N

Nantgaredig	II-109
Nantgarw Colliery	I-76, V-78
Nantgarw (PCN)	V-96
Nantybwch	I-24, IV-104, 105
Nantyderry	IV-82
Nantyffyllon	V-192
Nantyglo	I-1, 18, 19, IV-130, VI-16
Nantymoel	I-115, VI-148
Narberth	II-124
Neath	
- Abbey	III-141
- & Brecon Junction	I-168, VI-69
- Canalside branch	III-137
- Engine Shed	VI-110
- General	III-165, 166, VI-44
- Junction (R&SB)	III-134, 136
- Junction (VoN)	VI-43
- Riverside	I-167, VI-J
- shed (GW)	III-138, VI-111, 112
- shed (N&B)	I-168
Nelson	VI-22
Nelson & Llancaiach	VI-21, 23
Netherhope	IV-58
New Tredegar	I-45, 46
Newbridge	I-11
Newcastle Emlyn	II-107

Newlands	VI-122	Pembrey	II-74
Newport		Pembrey & Burry Port	II-1, 83
- Alexandra Dock Junction	III-17	Pembrey East	VI-89, 91, 92
- Cashmore's yard	III-9	Pembroke	II-134
- Courtybella Junction	IV-157, 158	Pembroke Dock	II-135, 136
- Dock Street	IV-160	Penallt	IV-65
- Dock Street shed	III-10, VI-186	Penalltau Junction	VI-19
- East Dock Junction	III-8	Penally	II-129
- Ebbw Junction	III-18	Penar Junction	I-150, 151, IV-175
- Ebbw Junction shed	III-19, 20, 21	Penarth	III-50
- Gaer Junction	IV-40	Penarth Dock	III-47, 48
- High Street	III-14, 15, IV-41, 161, VI-1	Pencader	II-103
- Iron Gates Crossing	III-13	- Junction	II-104
- Loco Yard Junction	III-12	Pencoed	III-103, VI-151
- Maesglas Junction	IV-156	Pengam Glam	V-113
- Maindee North Junction	IV-10	Pengam Mon	I-43, IV-167
- Mendalgief East	III-7	Penmaen	IV-176
- Mendalgief West	VI-190, 191	Penpergwm	IV-83
- Mill Street	IV-11	Penrhiwceiber High Level	I-155, VI-28
- Pill Bank Junction	IV-159	Penrhiwceiber Low Level	V-24
- Pill shed	III-J, 2, 3	Penrhos Junction	V-94, 95
- tunnel	III-16	Penscynor	I-169
Neyland	II-156, 159	Pentrebach	V-5
- shed	II-157, 158	Pentrepiod	IV-31
Nine Mile Point	IV-118	Pentwyn	IV-32
North Rhondda	I-139, 140	Pentwynmawr	IV-177
North's Collieries	I-128	Pentyrch Crossing	V-57
Nottage	III-112, 113	Penydarren	V-14
		Penygraig	I-104
O		Penyrheol	V-102, 159
Oakwood Junction	VI-59	Penywern Junction	V-129
Ogilvie Colliery	V-145	Peterston	III-93
Ogilvie Village	V-146	Pochin Pits	IV-109
Ogmore Vale	I-116, V-178	Pont Lawrence	IV-117
Old Ynysybwl	V-31	Pont Lliw	II-17
Onllwyn	I-172, 173	Pontardawe	II-43
		Pontardulais	II-18, 48
P		Pontcynon Bridge	V-22
Pandy	IV-89	Ponthenry	II-80
Pant	I-100, 101, 102	Ponthir	IV-8
Panteg & Coedygric Junction	IV-19, VI-8	Pontllanfraith High Level	I-152
Panteg & Griffithstown	IV-18	Pontllanfraith Low Level	IV-113
Pantyffordd	VI-76	Pontlottyn	I-59, V-121
Pantyffynnon	II-19, 20, IDX-5	Pontnewynydd	IV-26
- shed	II-117	- Junction	IV-23
Pantyscallog High Level	V-137	Pontrhydyfen	I-132, 133
Pantyscallog Low Level	V-130	Pontrhydyrun	IV-16
Pantywaun	V-141	Pontsarn for Vaynor	V-132
Park Junction	I-30, 31, IV-154, 155	Pontsticill Junction	V-136

13

Pontwalby VI-40
Pontyates II-79
Pontyberem II-81
Pontycymmer V-183
Pontypool
   - Blaendare Road IV-20
   - Clarence Street I-145
   - Crane Street IV-22
Pontypool Road IV-184
   - shed IV-2, 3
   - Station South IV-183
   - yards VI-9
Pontypridd I-78, 79, 80, V-1
   - Junction I-77, V-35, 36
   - PC&N Junction V-52
Pontypridd Graig V-156
Pontyrhyll V-182
   - Junction site VI-140
Porth V-40
Port Talbot
   - General III-124, 125, VI-125
   - West III-126
Port Talbot Central I-126
Porthcawl III-114, 115, 116, VI-115, 116
Portskewett IV-52
Puncheston II-167
Pwllyrhebog Junction V-47
Pyle III-J, 109, 117, VI-113, 117, 118
Pyle West III-118

Q
Quakers Yard High Level VI-26, 27
   - viaduct V-9
Quakers Yard Low Level V-8, VI-25

R
Radyr I-71, 72, 94, V-58, 59, VI-167, 168
   - shed I-69
Radyr Quarry Junction V-61
Raglan IV-74
Raglan Road Crossing IV-75
Red Lion Crossing II-30
Redbrook IV-66
Resolven I-163
Rhigos VI-38
   - Junction VI-39
Rhiwbina V-72
Rhiwderin I-117, IV-162
Rhondda Fach Junction V-44

Rhoose III-75
Rhydowen II-142
Rhymney I-58, 60, 61, V-122
Rhymney Bridge I-23, V-124, 125
Rhymney Lower IV-173
Risca IV-147, 148
   - Birds' yard I-10, IV-149
Roath Branch Junction V-65
Robertstown (site) IDX-3
Rogerstone I-9, IV-151, VI-11
Rosebush II-166

S
St. Athan III-78
St. Briavels IV-63
St. Clears II-120
St. Fagans III-92, VI-163
Sarnau II-119
Saundersfoot II-127
Sebastopol IV-17
Senghenydd I-54, 55
Seven Sisters I-170
Severn Tunnel Junction IV-46, 48, VI-3
   - East IV-50, VI-2, 5
   - shed IV-47
Sirhowy IV-106
Sirhowy Junction IV-174
Six Bells IV-134
Skewen III-167
   - East Junction III-168
Southerndown Road III-82, 83
Stormy Down III-1
Sudbrook IV-49
Sully II-41, III-55
Swanbridge III-54
Swansea
   - Burrows Sidings III-149
   - Cockett II-56
   - Copper Pit Platform II-10
   - Danygraig shed III-150
   - East Dock III-157
   - East Dock shed III-155, 156, VI-50
   - Eastern Depot Junction III-158
   - Hafod Junction II-4
   - High Street II-2, 3, III-174, 175, 176, VI-84, 85
   - King's Dock Junction III-148
   - Landore II-6, 7, 8
   - Landore shed II-5, III-172, 173
   - Loop East III-177

(Swansea)

- Loop West	VI-86
- Morriston	II-11, 45
- Pentrefelin	II-12
- Plas Marl	II-9
- Prince of Wales Dock Junction	III-151, VI-48
- Pritchard Siding	VI-47, 49
- Riverside	III-161
- St. Thomas	III-159
- Upper Bank	II-46, 47, VI-79, 80
- Wind Street Junction	III-164
- Victoria	II-118
Swansea Valley Junction	III-171

T

Taff Merthyr Colliery	I-174, 175
Taffs Well	I-73, 74, 75
Templeton	II-125
Tenby	II-128
Tidenham	IV-57
Tintern	IV-59, 60
Tir Phil	V-120
Tirydail	II-21
Tondu	I-111, V-186, 188, VI-141
- Middle Junction	I-109
- North Junction	VI-142, 144
- Ogmore Junction	V-185, VI-145
- shed	I-144
Tongwynlais	V-75
- tunnel	V-76
Tonteg Junction	V-154, 161
Tonygroes East	VI-131
Tonygroes West	VI-132
Tonypandy	V-46
Tonyrefail	V-169
Travellers Rest	V-34
Trecynon	VI-32
Tredegar	IV-107, 108
- shed	I-21
Tredegar Junction Lower	IV-114
Treforest	V-53
- Estate	V-55
- Junction	V-54
Treforest High Level	V-155
Treforest (PC&N)	V-98
Trehafod	V-39
- Junction	V-38
Treharris	I-154

Plate 7

The front end of 4-6-0 No.7903 Foremarke Hall on Landore shed.

20th June, 1953

Treherbert	I-84, 85
- shed	V-51
Trelewis Halt	VI-24
Trelewis Platform	V-17
Tremains	III-104
- Hayes' yard	I-129, III-105, VI-150
Treorchy	V-50
Treowen	IV-179
Trerhyngyll and Maindy	III-98
Trethomas	I-39, IV-164, VI-J
Trevethin Junction	IV-29
Trevil	I-25, IV-103
Trimsaran Road	II-77
Troedyrhiew Garth	V-190, VI-143
Troedyrhiw	V-6, VI-165
Trosnant Junction	IV-21
Tutshill	IV-55
Tycoch	II-90
Tyllwyn	IV-122
Tylorstown	V-42
Tynycaeau Junction	V-150, 157
Tynycwm	IV-150

U

Undy	IV-45
Upper Boat (CR)	V-79
Upper Pontnewydd	IV-15
Usk	IV-78

V

Varteg	IV-35
Victoria	I-14, IV-124

W

Waenavon	IV-38
Walnut Tree Junction	V-56
Walnut Tree West	V-158
Waterhall Junction	V-62
Waterhall Sidings	VI-119, 120
Waterloo	V-89
Welsh Hook	II-172
Wenvoe	III-56, VI-161, 162
Whitchurch	V-73
White Hart	V-90, 91
Whitebrook	IV-64
Whitland	II-122, 137
- shed	II-123
Windsor Colliery	V-104
Windsor Passing Siding	I-88
Wolfs Castle	II-171
Wye Valley Junction	IV-56
Wyesham	IV-67
Wylie	IV-115
Wyndham	V-179

Y

Ynysddu	IV-116
Ynyshir	V-41
Ynysybwl	I-89
Ynysybwl New Road	V-30
Ystalyfera	II-42
Ystrad Mynach	V-106, 107, VI-20
- North Junction	V-108
Ystrad Rhondda	V-49
Ystradgynlais	VI-78

Abbreviations in the next column:

? indicates origin uncertain;
T indicates Title page

Miscellaneous

A company signal is a prominent feature:

Barry	III-J, 72, 83, VI-J, 161
Brecon & Merthyr	I-36, 117
Burry Port & Gwendraeth Valley	II-82
Great Western	I-J, II-J, II-T, 12, 136, 150, III-T, 144, 175, IV-J, T, 161, V-J, T, 150, VI-T
London Midland & Scottish	II-39, 40
Rhymney	I-52, V-110
Taff Vale	I-T, 94

A company signal box is a prominent feature:

Barry	III-58, 74, 76, 82, V-150, 152, 158
Brecon & Merthyr	I-40, IV-162, 166, V-136, 138
Burry Port & Gwendraeth Valley	II-79
Great Western	I-18, 45, 108, 146, 147, II-8, 12, 16, 17, 36, II-56, 58, 59, 101, 103, 105, 107, 116, 135, 141, 148, II-154, 162, 169, 178, III-7, 8, 18, 27, 44, 110, 118, III-126, 143, 164, 171, 173, IV-11, 23, 24, 43, 56, 71, IV-82, 139, 154, 156, 157, 174, 183, V-94, 167, V-174, 178, 185, VI-2, 6, 27, 39, 41, 43, 44, 47, 48, VI-86, 87, 94, 103, 104, 105, 114, 115, 120, 122, 144, 145, 165, 166, 190, 191, IDX-9, 11
London & North Western	IV-33, 37, V-131
Midland	II-40, 47, VI-80
Port Talbot	VI-128, 129, 130, 135
Rhondda & Swansea Bay	III-136, 146, VI-56, 66
Rhymney Railway	I-57, 119, III-33, V-83, 86, 92, 109, 116
Swansea Harbour Trust	III-148
Taff Vale	I-89, 92, 95, III-40, 43, 44, V-28, 35, 37, V-52, 54, 61, 62, 63, VI-25, 164

Lineside Furniture, Notices:

Cardiff Railway Gate Notice	I-47
GWR/RR Joint Bridge Notice	I-64
Great Western Railway old-style Milepost	IV-7
Llynvi & Ogmore Railway Gradient Post	I-122
?Llynvi & Ogmore Railway Milepost	III-108
?Monmouthshire Railway & Canal Co. Milepost	IV-153
?Newport, Abergavenny & Hereford Railway Milepost	IV-178
Rhymney Railway Distance Post	V-111

Trespass Notices:

- Barry Dock & Railways	III-68, V-153
- Burry Port & Gwendraeth Valley Railway	II-69
- LNWR/RR Joint	I-61
- Port Talbot Railway	III-122, VI-137
- Rhondda & Swansea Bay Railway	III-162
- Rhymney Railway	I-58, 118c
- Taff Vale Railway	I-93

Plate 8

Fresh out of the shops, 0-6-0PT No.6403, from Pontypool Road shed, was photographed at Barry.

5th August, 1956

List of Locomotives

The following is not intended to be a complete list of locomotives shown or mentioned in the text of the Steam in South Wales series. It seemed worthwhile, however, to make a subjective assessment of photographs that might afford useful information about a particular engine for research or modelling purposes. Thus, engines barely visible at the far end of a train, for example, are not indexed although the number might appear in the photograph caption.

The main list is of BR engines; at the end is a list of locomotives carrying industrial numbers.   c - denotes colour plate

35	VI-181	384	I-86	1340	III-5
36	III-30	397	I-90	1471	I-103, 104, V-169, VI-155, 156
44	I-72, VI-168	435	I-34	1507	III-3
66	I-70	666	VI-189	1607	II-91
204	VI-179	667	III-4	1611	VI-90, 91
211	III-29	1021	VI-107	1620	V-36
316	V-123	1029	II-122	1637	II-137
345	VI-171	1101	III-148, 149, 150, VI-51	1651	VI-92
347	I-68	1140	III-153	1665	II-71
361	V-18	1142	III-147	2008	III-62
364	I-87	1144	III-163	2168	VI-88
366	I-51	1151	VI-52	2196	II-75
370	I-77	1152	III-152	2197	II-72
376	V-67	1338	III-160	2198	VI-95

2218	I-30
2247	V-115
2263	II-123
2815	VI-4
2879	III-16
2884	IV-149
2945	VI-183
3103	IV-151
3177	IV-50
3401	I-119c
3612	VI-163
3627	I-154
3633	II-163
3641	II-22
3647	IV-148, 166
3654	II-155
3668	III-J, VI-113
3683	VI-7
3698	II-52
3706	VI-70

Plate 9

After passing over the Morriston branch, 0-6-0PT No.8789 and brake van join the Swansea District Line at Felin Fran West.

26th July, 1960

3712	I-15		
3726	IV-164		
3767	I-41		
3772	III-13		
3777	II-26, 27, 37, 38, 48		
3832	VI-3		
3864	III-139		
4082	III-117, 133		
4093	VI-151		
4099	III-166		
4109	I-10		
4122	II-128, 131		
4126	III-61		
4127	VI-114		
4130	I-19, IV-130, VI-116		
4132	II-134, 136		
4134	II-172, 174		
4137	IV-46		
4138	I-162		
4150	VI-192		
4152	I-59		
4161	V-82		
4169	I-152, VI-24		
4207	VI-172		
4215	IV-116		
4225	IV-47		
4236	III-119		
4252	VI-112		
4254	III-150		
4255	VI-45		
4256	I-141c	4988	VI-125
4275	I-161	5001	II-2
4276	I-112	5009	VI-53
4279	I-158	5013	II-58
4282	III-146	5027	II-3
4285	VI-15	5030	III-175
4286	II-55, III-1	5037	I-10
4292	I-141c	5051	III-172
4294	IV-136	5055	VI-5
4408	I-110	5067	III-177
4550	II-146	5069	III-15
4557	II-139, 146	5080	II-88
4558	II-143	5087	II-93
4589	I-53	5099	IV-41
4593	VI-16	5195	I-79
4621	I-169	5207	II-51, VI-112
4652	I-27, IV-144	5211	I-141c
4654	II-161	5213	II-6
4668	IV-1, VI-28	5217	I-2, VI-10
4669	V-178, VI-147	5224	VI-112
4671	I-44, 45	5226	I-J
4677	II-171, 173, 176	5233	IV-141
4695	I-137	5237	V-90
4916	II-119	5255	II-16
4917	III-14	5262	III-92
4927	II-61	5263	VI-36
4929	III-107	5324	II-158
4958	II-95	5353	II-92
4971	III-84, IV-45	5414	III-22
4983	IDX-2	5524	V-174

Plate 10

After withdrawal in March 1964, former S&D 2-8-0 No.53808 was sent for cutting up by Messrs. Woodham Bros. at Barry but survived for preservation.

2nd August, 1964

5527	II-147	5662	III-67	6413	VI-32
5529	II-142	5667	I-71	6416	I-24
5544	I-11	5671	I-48, 65, V-14	6423	V-128
5545	I-116, V-179, 188	5674	I-63, 65, VI-23	6426	I-20, IV-110, 113, 115
5549	II-127	5676	VI-25	6427	I-23, IV-91
5550	II-124	5677	V-53	6430	I-22
5560	II-126	5694	III-89	6433	I-96, 160, V-3, VI-34
5568	I-47	5696	V-15	6434	I-76, 150
5574	I-106	5752	I-6, IV-28	6435	I-67, III-91, V-66
5600	I-81	5778	VI-44	6438	III-36, 37, 42
5602	II-13, VI-87, 170	5903	II-149, 153, 154	6439	IV-60
5607	III-47	5908	II-179	6605	IV-181
5608	I-83, V-39	5918	IV-4	6606	V-J
5610	V-43	5938	VI-169	6613	VI-49
5611	V-1	5939	VI-172	6614	V-71
5612	II-63, VI-41	5946	VI-176	6619	I-88
5613	I-90	5961	II-67, 89, 151	6621	VI-42
5614	I-84, V-44	5971	VI-175	6622	I-78, VI-26
5615	I-49, V-141	5975	VI-126	6624	III-60, V-105
5620	I-17	6000	III-11	6628	IV-J, 184, V-151, VI-37
5624	I-143c	6018	III-85	6634	I-142c
5631	III-112, VI-115	6166	IV-48	6636	VI-158
5633	I-3, III-56	6348	III-93	6637	III-75
5636	I-62, V-59	6355	II-125	6643	III-57
5637	VI-160	6362	III-114	6651	I-155
5649	I-145	6402	I-54	6652	V-73
5653	V-118	6403	IV-27, IDX-8	6656	IV-135
5655	V-17	6408	V-4	6659	III-103
5656	I-132	6411	I-90	6660	III-59
5657	IV-152, V-42	6412	IV-57, 63, 185	6661	I-156, 157
				6662	VI-50
				6677	III-110
				6691	I-128
				6693	IV-180
				6725	III-2
				6739	III-J
				6741	II-41
				6762	II-46
				6767	VI-79
				6818	II-J, III-121
				6834	II-83
				6909	VI-117
				6946	IV-6
				7001	III-176
				7003	III-17, VI-149
				7009	II-1
				7012	III-86, VI-106
				7016	II-60
				7021	II-4
				7036	VI-1

Plate 11

The signal box at Abercynon, opened in 1932 to replace two TVR boxes.

13th March, 1964

7200	II-33	7829	II-100
7205	V-60	7903	VI-178, IDX-7
7206	VI-14	8102	II-94
7210	VI-6	8104	I-85, VI-67
7220	IV-85	8414	III-129, IDX-J
7226	III-140	8420	V-78
7230	I-14, III-154, VI-110	8436	IV-121, 124
7231	VI-13	8444	VI-30
7237	III-17, VI-12	8445	I-165
7244	VI-136	8460	I-81
7245	III-21	8478	I-74
7246	I-9	8483	I-166
7248	VI-109	8490	VI-184
7249	VI-96	8497	VI-185
7306	II-162	8498	I-111, 123, III-107, V-190
7320	I-146, II-63, VI-187	8708	II-28, VI-102
7423	I-163	8736	I-99, 102
7439	II-108	8740	I-108, 109, V-188
7718	II-60	8775	I-172
7732	VI-143	8777	II-113
7739	VI-111	8782	III-136
7766	I-98	8784	VI-111
7771	IV-167	8785	II-49
7787	IV-163, 171	8786	I-1
7808	III-35, VI-174	9451	I-144c
7816	II-159	9475	VI-40
7818	II-102	9482	I-4, 5
7825	II-103	9485	III-169
7826	II-120	9607	VI-29

9609	V-180
9616	IV-165
9618	V-5, V-6
9642	I-129
9645	II-109, 169
9649	VI-142
9652	II-160
9660	I-144c
9661	I-39
9662	IV-9
9675	I-99, 100
9677	II-170
9735	VI-56
9737	VI-54
9746	IV-158
9783	I-167
9788	II-24
9792	VI-111
30545	II-53
40145	IV-95
42307	II-20
42388	II-116
45190	II-115
45283	II-21
45577	II-118
46508	V-142
47479	I-171
49064	I-57
49121	III-69, VI-157
49168	IV-99
49226	II-62
49409	III-71, VI-162
53807	VI-188
53808	IDX-10
82033	VI-62
82037	VI-167
82039	III-46
82042	VI-165
90572	IV-42
92004	I-12, 13
92209	IV-128

Miscellaneous engines

D3437	III-121
Ex-TVR 28 as NCB No.67	I-120c
M- Wardle Works No.1057	IV-12
H-Clarke Works No.1498	I-175
V-Foundry Works No.5272	I-121c
R Stephenson & Hawthorns Works No.6957 as RTB No.67	I-25